What greater thing is there for two human souls than to feel that they are joined for life?

George Eliot

Blue Mountain Arts®

"The Language of the Heart..." series

For an Amazing Son

Marriage Is a Promise to Love

Mothers & Daughters

A Sister Is Forever

To a Beautiful Daughter

True Friendship Is a Gift

The Language of the Heart...

Marriage Is a Promise to Love

A Blue Mountain Arts Collection

Edited by Patricia Wayant

Blue Mountain Press™

Boulder, Colorado

Library of Congress Control Number: 2019900048
ISBN: 978-1-68088-292-6

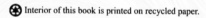 and Blue Mountain Press are registered in U.S. Patent and Trademark Office.
Certain trademarks are used under license.

Acknowledgments appear on the last page.

Handmade paper used on cover made in Thailand.
Printed and assembled in China.
First Printing: 2019

Interior of this book is printed on recycled paper.

Blue Mountain Arts, Inc.
P.O. Box 4549, Boulder, Colorado 80306

Contents

(Authors listed in order of first appearance)

Marriage
Is a Promise
to Love

The secrets to a happy marriage are to:

Love constantly and always be sweethearts.

Put each other first and honor each
    other's dreams.

Hug often and be thankful for everything
    you have.

Hope together and take special care
    of each other.

Show your respect by being thoughtful
    and generous with your praise.

Don't be afraid to cry in front of each other
    <u>for</u> each other.

Be truthful, listen with your heart, and
    laugh together.

Resolve hurt feelings, forgive quickly,
    and don't hold on to resentment.

Be mindful and considerate of each
    other's insecurities.

Don't give up on your marriage — ever!

♡ Donna Fargo

Marriage Is...

A commitment. Its success doesn't depend on feelings, circumstances, or moods — but on two people who are loyal to each other and the vows they took on their wedding day.

Hard work. It means chores, disagreements, misunderstandings, and times when you might not like each other very much. When you work at it together, it can be the greatest blessing in the world.

A relationship where two people must listen, compromise, and respect. It's an arrangement that requires a multitude of decisions to be made together. Listening, respecting, and compromising go a long way toward keeping peace and harmony.

A union in which two people learn from their mistakes, accept each other's faults, and willingly adjust behaviors that need to be changed. It's caring enough about each other to work through disappointing and hurtful times and believing in the love that brought you together in the first place.

Patience and forgiveness. It's being open and honest, thoughtful and kind. Marriage means talking things out, making necessary changes, and forgiving each other. It's unconditional love at its most understanding and vulnerable — love that supports, comforts, and is determined to triumph over every challenge and adversity.

Marriage is a partnership of two unique people who know that even though they are wonderful as individuals… they are even better together.

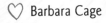 Barbara Cage

We Are Not Meant to Go Through Life Alone

We need a partner in life who will
forever remain by our side —
someone to lean on at times,
remembering, as well,
that we will be leaned on, too;
someone to share our joy
and hold us in sorrow.

Understand that there will be difficult times,
and doubt may cloud your lives.
It is then that you must
trust each other the most
and believe that love will sustain you.
Do not give up easily;
fight for what is most precious —
your marriage.
Help it survive
by nurturing it every single day.

Never hesitate to say "I love you"
or be the first one to say "I'm sorry."
Give a lot,
overlook even more,
and always expect as much in return.
Never look back
or lose yourself,
but celebrate the special privilege
of being a couple.
Never lose sight
of what brought you to the altar
in the first place:
your special love for each other.
Cherish that always.

Linda Hersey

Together in Marriage

Together in marriage
you will bring out the best
in each other
You will learn from each other
and grow from your differences
You will be two individuals
living your own lives
with each other as one

Together in marriage
you will be stronger
more sensitive
more aware, more knowing
and more at peace
than you are individually
You will be better people

Together in marriage
your love will give understanding
to all that you do
because you will share
your ideas, goals
and frustrations
And you will always have
someone to support
whatever you say and do

Together in marriage
you will be able
to achieve
all that you want
in life

 Susan Polis Schutz

All I Know About Love

This is everything I have to tell you about love: *nothing*.
This is everything I've learned about marriage: *nothing*.

Only that the world out there is complicated,
and there are beasts in the night, and delight and pain,
and the only thing that makes it okay, sometimes,
is to reach out a hand in the darkness and find another
    hand to squeeze,
and not to be alone.

It's not the kisses, or never just the kisses: it's what
    they mean.
Somebody's got your back.
Somebody knows your worst self and somehow
    doesn't want to rescue you
or send for the army to rescue them.

It's not two broken halves becoming one.
It's the light from a distant lighthouse bringing you
    both safely home
because home is wherever you are both together.

So this is everything I have to tell you about love and
     marriage: *nothing,*
like a book without pages or a forest without trees.

Because there are things you cannot know before you
     experience them.
Because no study can prepare you for the joys or
     the trials.
Because nobody else's love, nobody else's marriage,
     is like yours,
and it's a road you can only learn by walking it,
a dance you cannot be taught,
a song that did not exist before you began, together,
     to sing.

And because in the darkness you will reach out a hand,
not knowing for certain if someone else is even there.
And your hands will meet,
and then neither of you will ever need to be alone again.

 Neil Gaiman

When Two Become One

When two people join together and bond their lives forever because they are certain they have something special that will make their marriage last… this is the first act of faith.

Upon this act of faith, these two people will build a life. And as long as their determination stays with them, this life will always be their hope, their dream, their truth, their being, their inspiration, and their source of strength.

Through their life together, they will hurt and laugh. Together, they will feel all of life's ups and downs. They will learn and grow through trial and error. The lessons will show them the meaning of true love and the difference between a love that lasts and one that just gives up.

These two people will face each failure together and discover the strength to go on. They will encourage each other's dreams and forgive each other's faults.

Through a labor of love, these two will become as one — fighting against the odds and ultimately creating a marriage that will grow into an infinite love.

♡ Regina Riddle

This Marriage

May these vows and this marriage
    be blessed.
May it be sweet milk,
this marriage, like wine and halvah.
May this marriage offer fruit and shade
like the date palm.
May this marriage be full of laughter,
our every day a day in paradise.
May this marriage be a sign of
    compassion,
a seal of happiness here and hereafter.
May this marriage have a fair face and a
    good name,
an omen as welcome
as the moon in a clear blue sky.
I am out of words to describe
how spirit mingles in this marriage.

♡ Rumi

I dreamed of a wedding of elaborate elegance; a church filled with flowers and friends. I asked him what kind of wedding he wished for; he said one that would make me his wife.

♡ Author Unknown

I'm here forever as your husband, best friend and supporter, love and life partner. The vows we exchanged are not merely words; they are me and everything I hope to be. They are a part of my love, a part of my soul, and forever a part of my heart.

♡♡ Tim M. Krzys

From this day forward,
you shall not walk alone.
My heart will be your shelter,
and my arms will be your home.

♡ Author Unknown

In marriage, many days will bring happiness, while other days may be sad. But together, two hearts can overcome everything.

All of the moments won't be exciting or romantic, and sometimes worries and anxiety will be overwhelming. But together, two hearts that accept will find comfort.

Recollections of past joys, pains, and shared feelings will be the glue that holds everything together during even the worst and most insecure moments.

Reaching out to each other as a friend, and becoming the confidant and companion that the other one needs, is the true magic and beauty of any two people together.

It's inspiring in each other a dream or a feeling, and having faith in each other and not giving up… even when all the odds say to quit.

It's allowing each other to be vulnerable, to be himself or herself, even when the opinions or thoughts aren't in total agreement or exactly what you'd like them to be.

It's getting involved and showing interest in each other, really listening and being available, the way any best friend should be.

Exactly three things need to be remembered in a marriage if it is to be a mutual bond of sharing, caring, and loving throughout life: love, trust, and forgiveness.

♡ Regina Riddle

Advice to the Young on Their Wedding Day

Marriage is about the long, slow journey: the moments, simple daily moments.... It's about letting each other do the things that make you crazy. Don't argue over the little things like how she lets knives dry in the drying rack tips up or how much you hate that old, worn out pair of pants he's owned for fifteen years. When he tells you the same story for the fiftieth time, and each time it's gotten more fanciful, smile, nod, and tell him what a great story it is. There are just some things men and women will never fix in each other. And they may best be left unfixed.

Rather than trying to change each other, learn to love each other for exactly who you each are. Be honest with each other, even if it hurts.

Argue. Challenge each other. Push each other to do good and be better. Know that the baggage and issues you each bring into this partnership don't magically disappear on your wedding day. In fact, they'll most likely intensify. Be prepared to battle not only your own demons in the years to come, but each other's.

Laugh. Laugh as much as possible, at yourself and each other. But always laugh at yourself first. It's unfair and unkind to laugh at others if you haven't first proven yourself to be an equal or greater fool.

Find your balance with each other. To use a sports analogy, you need a starting pitcher and a closer. My wife knows that it may take me years to start a household project. But if she starts it — painting a room or tearing up the hideous green carpet in the living room — I can't help but jump in to see it through. If she doesn't do her part, the job will never get started. If I don't do mine, it will never get done… right.

Long after the honeymoon, take time each day to remember the feeling that brought you together on your wedding day — that magical sense of knowing that this was the person you've been waiting for all these years. The feeling that isolated you two from the rest of the world and made you pity everyone else, for surely no one else has ever felt a love, knowing, and joy like this before. Keep that feeling for yourselves like a firefly in a jar and put it up on your dresser. Bring it down at least once each day, open it up for a moment and remember.

 Patrick Caneday

Made for Each Other

When you find somebody you love, all the way through, and she loves you — even with your weaknesses, your flaws, everything starts to click into place. And if you can talk to her, and she listens, if she makes you laugh, and makes you think, makes you want, makes you see who you really are, and who you are is better, just better with her, you'd be crazy not to want to spend the rest of your life with her.

♡ Nora Roberts

We were meant to be.
We were made for each other.
Just as the ocean was made
    to reflect the sunset,
    the stars to answer wishes,
    and dreams to carry hope,
so was our love made
    for a special purpose.

♡♡ Barbara Lynn

The moment I will never forget is… standing at the altar as my wife came down the aisle. I was overcome by a sense of calm that was very indicative of what a great decision it was.

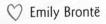 Steve Carell

I can't believe it
Out of all the millions of people
in hundreds of countries
and thousands of cities
I was able to find
my true heart
my true soul
my true love

♡ Susan Polis Schutz

Whatever our souls are made of, his and mine are the same.

♡ Emily Brontë

What It's like to Love You

To love you is to daydream of you often, think of you so much, speak of you proudly, and miss you terribly when we are apart.

To love you is to cherish the warmth of your arms, the sweetness of your kisses, the friendliness of your smile, the loving sound in your voice, and the happiness we share.

To love you is to not forget the adversity we have overcome, the tears we have shed, the plans we have made, the problems we have solved, and the pain of separation.

To love you is to remember joyfully the days we made memorable, the moments that will live forever in our hearts, the dreams we hope for, the feelings we have for each other, the caresses and touches of love, and the exhilaration of love that fills our hearts.

To love you is to need you, want you, hold you, and know you as no one else can.

To love you is to realize that life without you would be no life at all.

♡ Daniel Haughian

The Art of Marriage

Happiness in marriage is not something that just happens. A good marriage must be created. In the art of marriage the *little things* are the *big things*...

It is never being too old to hold hands.

It is remembering to say, "I love you," at least once each day.

It is never going to sleep angry.

It is at no time taking the other for granted; the courtship shouldn't end with the honeymoon, it should continue through all the years.

It is having a mutual sense of values and common objectives; it is standing together facing the world.

It is forming a circle of love that gathers in the whole family.

It is doing things for each other, not in the attitude of duty or sacrifice, but in the spirit of joy.

It is speaking words of appreciation and demonstrating gratitude in thoughtful ways.

It is not expecting the husband to wear a halo or the wife to have the wings of an angel. It is not looking for perfection in each other. It is cultivating flexibility, patience, understanding, and a sense of humor.

It is having the capacity to forgive and forget.

It is giving each other an atmosphere in which each can grow.

It is finding room for the things of the spirit. It is a common search for the good and the beautiful.

It is not only marrying the right partner, it is *being* the right partner.

Wilferd A. Peterson

Marriage Is...

...a commitment to life — to the best that two people can find and bring out in each other. It offers opportunities for sharing and growth no other human relationship can equal, a physical and emotional joining that is promised for a lifetime.

♡ Edmund O'Neill

...a mutual trust and a vow you renew daily. It's putting each other first in the little things that matter a lot and the big things that help two people grow together. It's the promise you keep living up to, and it lasts forever and ever.

♡♡ Donna Fargo

...two souls with but a single thought, two hearts that beat as one.

♡ Friedrich Halm

…the joining of two people who share the promise that only marriage can make — to share the sunshine and the shadows, and to experience a richer, more fulfilling life because of it.

♡ Bettie Meeks

…a spiritual partnership and union in which we willingly give and receive love, create and share intimacy, and open ourselves to be available and accessible to another human being in order to heal, learn, and grow.

♡ Iyanla Vanzant

…a promise to stay together, to dream together, to work on whatever needs attention, to keep love fresh and alive, and to continue to bless the beauty of your lives.

♡ Douglas Pagels

…a journey that leads to great love.

♡ Mary E. Buddingh

$\mathcal{A}$ happy marriage does more than stand the test of time. It causes two lives to sail toward eternity in each other's arms, learning lessons they couldn't learn alone or with anyone else. It's the source of joy that gives every day its smile. It's two sweethearts for life sharing dreams and trying to make them come true. Marriage is a celebration of eager promises and an endless number of beautiful tomorrows and happy anniversaries ever after.

♡ Donna Fargo

$\mathcal{W}$hat counts in making a happy marriage is not so much how compatible you are, but how you deal with incompatibility.

♡ Leo Tolstoy

You go home. You find little things to cherish. You have a favorite chair. You develop a coffee ritual, a storybook ritual, some running jokes. From little things emerges something big, and you realize that being married with kids is the essential condition of your life, an immutable fact, something you don't ever want to change.

Just like true love.

♡ Joel Achenbach

A happy marriage is a long conversation which always seems too short.

♡ André Maurois

The highest happiness on earth is marriage.

♡ William Lyon Phelps

A Marriage

You are holding up a ceiling
with both arms. It is very heavy,
but you must hold it up, or else
it will fall down on you. Your arms
are tired, terribly tired,
and, as the day goes on, it feels
as if either your arms or the ceiling
will soon collapse.

But then, unexpectedly,
something wonderful happens:
Someone, a man or a woman,
walks into the room
and holds their arms up
to the ceiling beside you.

So you finally get
to take down your arms.
You feel the relief of respite,
the blood flowing back
to your fingers and arms.
And when your partner's arms tire,
you hold up your own
to relieve him again.

And it can go on like this
for many years
without the house falling.

♡ Michael Blumenthal

Love Poem

The afternoon we left our first apartment,
we scrubbed it down from ceiling to parquet.
Who knew the place could smell like lemon muffins?
It suddenly seemed nuts to move away.

The morning someone bought our station wagon,
it gleamed with wax and every piston purred.
That car looked like a centerfold in *Hot Rod!*
Too late, we saw that selling was absurd.

And then there was the freshly tuned piano
we passed along to neighbors with a wince.
We told ourselves we'd find one even better;
instead we've missed its timbre ever since.

So if, God help us, we are ever tempted
to ditch our marriage when it's lost its glow,
let's give the thing our finest spit and polish —
and, having learned our lesson, not let go.

 Melissa Balmain

Marriage Is Two People Sharing Everything in Life

In marriage
two people share
all their dreams and goals
their weaknesses and strengths
In marriage
two people share
all the joys and sadnesses of life
and all the supreme pleasures
In marriage
two people share
all of their emotions and feelings
all of their tears and laughter

Marriage is the most
fulfilling relationship
one can have
and the love that you share
as husband and wife
is beautifully forever

♡ Susan Polis Schutz

Sometimes I think, *If I were to do my wedding today, I would do things differently.* With everything I've learned, the places I've gone, the design ideas I've seen, I would want to include all sorts of details that I never could have even imagined back then.

But then I flip open our wedding album and see the smiling faces of the people we love all gathered in that place where we chose to celebrate our special day together…. Everything we cared about was exactly the way we wanted. When I look back, I realize I wouldn't change a single thing.

 Joanna Gaines

From every human being there rises a light that reaches straight to heaven. And when two souls that are destined to be together find each other, their streams of light flow together, and a single brighter light goes forth from their united being.

♡ Baal Shem Tov

It Won't Always Be Easy

Marriage does not promise that there will
not be any rough times,
just the assurance that there will
always be someone who cares
and who will help you through
to better times.
Marriage does not promise eternal romance,
just eternal love and commitment.
Marriage can't prevent disappointments,
disillusionment, or grief,
but it can offer hope, acceptance,
and comfort.

♡ Bettie Meeks

Love is difficult. For one human being to love
another is perhaps the most difficult task of all,
the epitome, the ultimate test. It is that striving
for which all other striving is merely preparation.

♡ Rainer Maria Rilke

Habitation

Marriage is not
a house or even a tent

it is before that, and colder:

the edge of the forest, the edge
of the desert
              the unpainted stairs
at the back where we squat
outside, eating popcorn

the edge of the receding glacier

where painfully and with wonder
at having survived even
this far

we are learning to make fire

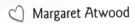 Margaret Atwood

In order to have a successful marriage
you must put out of your mind
any lessons learned
from previous relationships
because if you carry a sensitivity
     or fear with you
you won't be acting freely
and you won't let yourself
     be really known

In order to have a successful marriage
it is essential that both people
be completely open and honest

♡ Susan Polis Schutz

Learn the wisdom of compromise,
for it is better to bend a little than to break.

♡ Jane Wells

Work slowly with each other and build a relationship that you both can enjoy being a part of.

Share love and understand that neither of you is perfect; you are both subject to human frailties.

Encourage each other to pursue your dreams, even when you're weary from trying.

Expect the best that you both have to give, and still love when you fall short of your expectations.

Be friends; respect each other's individual personality, and give each other room to grow.

Be candid with each other, and point out strengths and weaknesses.

Understand each other's personal philosophy, even if you don't agree.

Be friends as well as lovers.

 Denise Braxton-Brown

On Marriage

Let there be spaces in your togetherness,
And let the winds of heaven dance between you.

Love one another, but make not a bond of love:
Let it rather be a moving sea between the shores of
  your souls.
Fill each other's cup but drink not from one cup.
Give one another of your bread but eat not from the
  same loaf.
Sing and dance together and be joyous, but let each
  one of you be alone,
Even as the strings of a lute are alone though they
  quiver with the same music.

Give your hearts, but not into each other's keeping.
For only the hand of Life can contain your hearts.
And stand together yet not too near together:
For the pillars of the temple stand apart,
And the oak tree and the cypress grow not in each
  other's shadow.

♡ Kahlil Gibran

A good relationship has a pattern like a dance and is built on some of the same rules. The partners do not need to hold on tightly, because they move confidently in the same pattern, intricate but gay and swift and free, like a country dance of Mozart's. To touch heavily would be to arrest the pattern and freeze the movement, to check the endlessly changing beauty of its unfolding. There is no place here for the possessive clutch, the clinging arm, the heavy hand; only the barest touch in passing. Now arm in arm, now face to face, now back to back — it does not matter which. Because they know they are partners moving to the same rhythm, creating a pattern together, and being invisibly nourished by it.

♡ Anne Morrow Lindbergh

Remember the Promise of Your Wedding Vows

True love is never perfect.
You will argue, fight, complain,
   and blame.
But the promise of
your wedding vows —
to love, honor, and cherish
   each other —
overcomes all your conflicts
and reminds you to stop
   and count your blessings.

Your love is as strong
as the promise you made
to each other
the day you were married.

And in the turbulence
of the worst storms,
your true love
will always stand tall.

You will keep on surviving
and thriving
in your garden of real-life
      togetherness.
And the beautiful thing
is that you will not only survive,
but bloom magnificently —
because you are
always in love with each other.

 Jacqueline Schiff

A Walled Garden

Your marriage should have within it a secret and protected space, open to you alone. Imagine it to be a walled garden, entered by a door to which only you have the key. Within this garden you will cease to be a mother, father, employee, homemaker, or any of the other roles which you fulfill in daily life. Here you are yourselves, two people who love each other. Here you can concentrate on one another's needs. So take each other's hands and go forth to your garden. The time you spend together is not wasted but invested — invested in your future and the nurture of your love.

♡ Author Unknown

Marriage is a bridge that allows the love of two very special people to give meaning and worth and wonder to life. It is a continual process of building; of shaping; of communicating; and caring. It is the deepest and sweetest understanding. It is sharing todays and tomorrows together and making each one more treasured and more complete than anyone could make them alone. A marriage is a home interwoven with hopes and memories and dreams. The thankfulness and love it can bring have no comparison. It is the most beautiful thing that can happen… to anyone.

♡ Collin McCarty

The question is asked: "Is there anything more beautiful in life than a young couple clasping clean hands and pure hearts in the path of marriage? Can there be anything more beautiful than young love?"

And the answer is given: "Yes, there is a more beautiful thing. It is the spectacle of an old man and an old woman finishing their journey together on that path. Their hands are gnarled but still clasped; their faces are seamed but still radiant; their hearts are physically bowed and tired but still strong with love and devotion. Yes, there is a more beautiful thing than young love. Old love."

♡ Author Unknown

Like life, marriage changes. It grows. It expands. When we fell in love, life was more carefree with less responsibility. We had time to learn about each other. It was a time when we embraced more risk and embarked on new adventures. We had time to watch each other grow.

Gradually, we grew closer and closer, learning what makes the other tick. We learned truly important things, like compassion and understanding. We learned how to care for each other's feelings.

We learned that marriage is about family and working together as a team. It's respecting each other and bringing the best of ourselves to the marriage.

♡ Kathryn Leibovich

Love seems the swiftest, but it is the slowest of all growths. No man or woman really knows what perfect love is until they have been married a quarter of a century.

♡ Mark Twain

"Marry Me"

a senryu sequence

When I come late to bed
I move your leg flung over my side —
that warm gate

nights you're not here
I inch toward the middle
of this boat, balancing

when I turn over in sleep
you turn, I turn, you turn,
I turn, you

some nights you tug the edge
of my pillow under your cheek,
look in my dream

pulling the white sheet
over your bare shoulder
I marry you again

 Veronica Patterson

Marriage is never forgetting
the day your love first began;
it's recalling that first glance
and the way you felt
when your eyes first met.
It's about holding on to
the sincerity and closeness you felt
when learning and discovering
each other for the first time.
But most importantly,
marriage is a choice and a commitment
to bring good into each other's lives,
and to always have faith
as you travel through
the years together.

♡ Lisa Mae Huddleston

Grow old along with me!
The best is yet to be.

♡♡ Robert Browning

The Most Beautiful Commitment of All

What greater thing is there for two human souls than to feel that they are joined for life?

♡ George Eliot

The most wonderful of all things in life, I believe, is the discovery of another human being with whom one's relationship has a glowing depth, beauty, and joy as the years increase. This inner progressiveness of love between two human beings is a most marvelous thing; it cannot be found by looking for it or by passionately wishing for it. It is a sort of Divine accident.

♡ Hugh Walpole

In marriage
you make the most beautiful
commitment in life —
to love each other forever
You will share
work and play
happiness and sadness
goals and values
family and friends
excitement and boredom
You will build a life
which is stronger because
you are now part of a team —
a team which should go through life
holding hands
always cheering for each other
In marriage
you make the most beautiful
commitment in life —
two people
in love
joining together
to become
one forever

♡ Susan Polis Schutz

Marriage Is
a Promise for Life

Marriage is made in heaven and nourished on earth. It is cultivated with loving kindness, mutual politeness, and hearts entwined in intimacy.

Marriage is full of wonderful times shared and bad times survived. It is supporting, praising, and communicating with confidence and positive expectations.

Marriage is laughing together in the sunshine, crying together in the rain, and never letting a day go by without showing your appreciation for each other. It is a partnership of hard work with a healthy balance of playful companionship.

Marriage is full of sunrises and sunsets shared in the haven of each other's arms. It's making decisions with attention to each other's needs. It's attentive listening and respect. It's helping your partner reach personal goals. It's a team effort of growing the relationship, building a family, and meeting the day-to-day challenges.

Marriage is dedicated to sustaining a loving relationship for the rest of your days. It is the fulfillment of your promise to love, honor, and cherish your partner and walk hand in hand into your twilight years.

♥♥ Jacqueline Schiff

Acknowledgments

We gratefully acknowledge the permission granted by the following authors, publishers, and authors' representatives to reprint poems or excerpts in this publication: PrimaDonna Entertainment Corp. for "The Secrets to a Happy Marriage," "...a mutual trust...," and "A happy marriage..." by Donna Fargo. Copyright © 2010, 2017 by PrimaDonna Entertainment Corp. All rights reserved. Writers House LLC, acting as agent for the author, for "All I Know About Love" from "Wedding Thoughts," *journal.neilgaiman* (blog), October 22, 2017, http://journal.neilgaiman.com/2017/10/wedding-thoughts-all-i-know-about-love.html. Copyright © 2017 by Neil Gaiman. All rights reserved. The Permissions Company, Inc., on behalf of Shambhala Publications, Inc., Boulder, Colorado, www.shambhala.com, for "This Marriage" by Rumi, from THE POCKET RUMI, translated by Kabir Helminski. Copyright © 2001 by Kabir Edmund Helminski. All rights reserved. Patrick Caneday for "Advice to the Young on Their Wedding Day" by Patrick Caneday, *The Good Men Project* (blog), November 15, 2012, https://goodmenproject.com/featured-content/the-good-life-advice-to-the-young-on-their-wedding-day/. Copyright © 2012 by Patrick Caneday. All rights reserved. Berkley, an imprint of Penguin Publishing Group, a division of Penguin Random House LLC, and Little, Brown Book Group Limited for "When you find somebody to love..." from VISION IN WHITE by Nora Roberts. Copyright © 2009 by Nora Roberts. All rights reserved. Steve Carell for "The moment I will never forget..." from "Man of the House: Steve Carell" by Cortney Pellettieri, *Good Housekeeping*, August 7, 2012, https://www.goodhousekeeping.com/life/inspirational-stories/interviews/a19538/steve-carell-interview/. Copyright © 2012 by Steve Carell. All rights reserved. Judy Shepherd for "The Art of Marriage" from THE ART OF LIVING by Wilferd A. Peterson. Copyright © 1960, 1961 by Wilferd A. Peterson. All rights reserved. ESSENCE Communications, Inc. for "...a spiritual partnership..." from "Iyanla Vanzant Answers Your Questions" by Iyanla Vanzant, *Essence*, January 17, 2013, https://www.essence.com/news/iyanla-vanzant-answers-your-questions/. Copyright © 2013 by Iyanla Vanzant. All rights reserved. Don Congdon Associates, Inc. for "You go home..." from "Homeward Bound" by Joel Achenbach, published in HERE LIES MY HEART, Beacon Press 1999. Copyright © 1997 by Joel Achenbach. All rights reserved. Michael Blumenthal for "A Marriage" from AGAINST ROMANCE. Copyright © 1987 by Michael Blumenthal. All rights reserved. Able Muse Press for "Love Poem" from WALKING IN ON PEOPLE by Melissa Balmain. Copyright © 2014 by Melissa Balmain. All rights reserved. W Publishing, an imprint of Thomas Nelson, a division of HarperCollins Christian Publishing, Inc., for "Sometimes I think..." from THE MAGNOLIA STORY by Chip and Joanna Gaines. Copyright © 2016 by Chip and Joanna Gaines. All rights reserved. New World Library, Novato, CA, www.newworldlibrary.com, for "Love is difficult" from LETTERS TO A YOUNG POET by Rainer Maria Rilke. Copyright © 2000 by Rainer Maria Rilke. All rights reserved. Houghton Mifflin Harcourt Publishing Company for "Habitation" from SELECTED POEMS, 1965-1975 by Margaret Atwood. Copyright © 1976 by Margaret Atwood. All rights reserved. Pantheon Books, an imprint of the Knopf Doubleday Publishing Group, a division of Penguin Random House LLC, for "A good relationship..." from "Argonauta" from GIFT FROM THE SEA by Anne Morrow Lindbergh. Copyright © 1955, 1975, copyright renewed 1983 by Anne Morrow Lindbergh. All rights reserved. New York University Press for "Marry Me" from SWAN, WHAT SHORES? by Veronica Patterson. Copyright © 2000 by New York University. All rights reserved. Lisa Mae Huddleston for "Marriage is never forgetting...." Copyright © 2019 by Lisa Mae Huddleston. All rights reserved.